Contents

LEARNING IS CHILD'S PLAY

Over 100 creative, learning activities for young children

Jan Morrow

Acknowledgements

To Keith who makes all things possible.
To Kate, Sophie and Nicholas, my inspiration!
To Liz Rashid, my playgroup colleague, for some of
the ideas in this book.

LONGMAN GROUP UK LIMITED,
Longman House, Burnt Mill, Harlow,
Essex CM20 2JE, England
and Associated Companies throughout the world.

First published 1987
Second impression 1987
ISBN 0 582 23623 1

Set in 11/12½pt Rockwell Light, Linotron 202

Printed and bound in Great Britain by
Butler & Tanner Ltd, Frome and London

Introduction

This book is designed to help parents and people looking after young children. It contains instructions for over 100 interesting activities which will involve the children in creative play, and help them to learn a wide variety of practical skills and concepts.

All the ideas described here have been successfully used with pre-school and reception class children. They are just as suitable for use in the home as they are in the playgroup or nursery school.

The aim is to encourage children to create; by doing this they will learn a whole range of skills and ideas – everything from how to hold a pair of scissors to the importance of washing your hands before you do some cooking.

There are ten sections in the book, containing activities of different kinds for different occasions. Each activity is self-contained so you can dip into the book wherever you choose.

As far as possible, everything should be done by the children themselves and adults should resist the temptation to 'tidy it up'. Even if the finished product looks very 'messy' to the grown-up eye, it doesn't matter. The important thing is for the model or picture to be the child's own work and for the child to enjoy being creative. Obviously adults must sometimes have an active role in measuring, cutting, drawing etc, but when you help, remember to involve the child as much as possible and talk about what you are doing and why. It is sometimes helpful to use templates (prepared shapes for the child to draw round) when the child needs to draw a specific shape, but don't over-use them because they can easily stifle the child's creativity.

As you can see from the following list, equipment for these activities need not be expensive.

Cardboard

This can be cut from empty cereal or washing-powder boxes. If very thick card is needed, grocery boxes from the supermarket are ideal. Small pieces of thin card can be taken from the back of old Christmas and birthday cards.

Material

Jumble sales provide marvellous scraps of material and wool.

Glue

For sticking paper on to paper, wallpaper paste is quite adequate. But do make sure that it doesn't contain fungicide – many do even if the packet doesn't actually say so. However, for most activities a good quality strong glue such as washable PVA medium is preferable. You can easily obtain this glue and fungicide-free paste from art shops or educational suppliers.

Paper

For activities such as hand printing, old newspaper can be used. When white paper is required, wallpaper lining paper is ideal. Used computer paper is also very useful and it is worth finding out if anyone you know can provide some.

Paint

Powder paint is less expensive than ready-mixed and lends itself to a greater number of activities as it can be made thick or thin. Always add a drop of washing-up liquid to mixed powder paint as this prevents it from flaking and makes washing paint out of clothes much easier. If you keep unused paint in a screw-top jar, it stops it drying out too quickly.

Junk boxes

Keep a large box or bag handy in the kitchen and put empty cardboard or plastic containers into it for use later. The moral is simple. Never throw anything away; your child can use it.

Safety

1 Remember to:

- stop little ones putting paint, varnish, glue etc into their mouths.

- train your children not to put scissors or sharp objects near their faces. Safety scissors are easily obtainable from good toy shops.

- tell the children to wash their hands before cooking and after activities using paint, varnish or glue.

- supervise carefully all cooking activities – especially when knives are being used. Obviously little ones must not be allowed to use the cooker or handle hot pans.

2 Remember **not** to:

- use dried red kidney beans. These are highly poisonous.

- use polystyrene containers or chips. They give off a fine dust and are dangerous if swallowed.

- let little ones use spray cans of varnish or paint. These should only be used by an adult in a very well-ventilated place.

Paper and card

Mr Long Legs

This is what you need:

- 1 paper plate.
- 2 strips of card 3cm by 40cm.
- Felt tip pens or crayons.
- Sellotape.
- Scissors.

Help the child to:

1 Draw a silly face on the paper plate.
2 Fold the strips of card like a concertina.

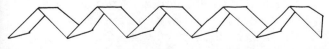

3 Attach the legs to the back of the plate with sellotape.

Make a jigsaw

This is what you need:

- Old magazines, comics or birthday/Christmas cards.
- Scissors.
- A piece of card the same size as the picture you choose.
- Glue and a glue brush.
- A pencil.
- A large envelope.

Help the child to:

1 Find a colourful picture and cut it out.
2 Stick the picture on to the card and when it is dry cut it into pieces. Obviously the younger the child the fewer the pieces. Cutting through card can be difficult for little ones, so you could omit the card altogether and just cut the picture.
3 Try to put the picture back together again and when you have finished pop the jigsaw into the envelope to keep safe until next time.

A paper snail

This is what you need:

- *1 strip of thin card, about 5cm by 50cm.*
- *Felt tip pens or crayons.*
- *Sellotape.*
- *1 drinking straw.*
- *Scissors.*

Help the child to:

1 Decorate both sides of the strip of card with patterns, scribble or bands of colour.

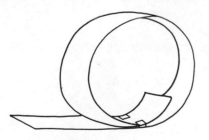

2 Loosely roll one end of the strip of card into a snail shell shape and then sellotape it into position.

3 Bend the flat end of the card to make a head and add two eyes with a felt tip pen. You can use two tiny pieces of straw sellotaped into position for feelers.
4 Why not have a snail race? Attach a length of cotton to each snail, twist the loose end of cotton round a pencil and pull the snails across a smooth table top by winding the cotton round the pencils. It'll never replace the Grand National, but it's good CLEAN fun.

A rabbit in a hutch

This is what you need:

- *A sheet of paper. A good size would be 30cm by 25cm.*
- *A triangle of thick brown cardboard taken from an empty grocery box. The triangle needs to be about 15cm by 15cm by 18cm.*
- *2 small balls of white cotton wool.*
- *Strong glue and a glue brush.*
- *Felt tip pens.*
- *A piece of plastic or string netting, 19cm by 11cm. The type of netting used for orange or peanut bags would be fine.*
- *A ruler.*

Help the child to:

1 Draw a rectangle 18cm by 10cm in the centre of the paper. This will be the hutch.
2 Make a roof for the hutch by sticking the cardboard triangle on top of the rectangle you have drawn.
3 Put the rabbit in the hutch by sticking the two balls of wool next to each other in the rectangle, and add eyes, ears and a tail with a felt tip pen.
4 Put the front on the hutch by sticking the netting into position. Trim the netting slightly if it seems too large. This is one rabbit that mum won't have to clean out.

Can-label lotto

This is what you need:

- *Some can labels. (Before you throw away any empty tin cans take the paper labels off them and start a collection. Collect together pairs of identical labels. If four children are going to play this game you will need 24 different pairs of labels.)*
- *One piece of thin card for every child wanting to play the game. A good size for the card would be 16cm by 24cm.*
- *Glue and a glue brush.*
- *A pencil and ruler.*
- *Scissors.*

Help the children to:

1 Divide each card into six equal sections by drawing lines with the pencil and ruler.

2 Take all the labels you have collected and sort them out into identical pairs e.g. two baked beans, two pineapple chunks etc.

3 Trim all the labels so that they fit snugly inside the marked squares on the cards. When cutting the labels, make sure that both labels in the same pair are trimmed identically.

4 Glue just one from each pair of labels into the marked sections on the cards. Do this until all the marked sections have a label in. You should be left with a pile of labels identical to the ones glued on to the cards.

5 To play the game each child has a card with six can labels stuck on it. The loose labels are turned face down. Each child takes it in turn to pick a label and try to match it with a label on her card. If it is identical she places it on top of the card label; if not, she returns it face down to the pile. The winner is the first one to cover all her labels.

Milk-top threading

This is what you need:

- *Lots of clean milk bottle tops.*
- *A ball of wool.*
- *A darning needle – the type which is large and blunt-ended.*
- *Scissors.*

Help the child to:

Thread the needle with wool. Tie a knot at the end and thread the milk tops on to the wool. Even very young children find it easy to "sew" milk bottle tops and the finished product could be turned into a necklace.

A paper frog

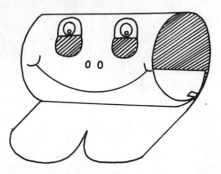

This is what you need:

- *A strip of green paper 20cm by 35cm.*
- *Felt tip pens or crayons.*
- *Sellotape.*
- *Scissors.*

Help the child to:

1 Draw the very simple outline of two frog's feet at one end of the piece of paper and cut round the outline.

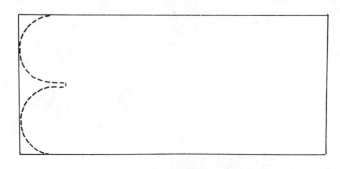

2 Take the uncut end of the paper, loosely roll it towards the feet and sellotape it into position.

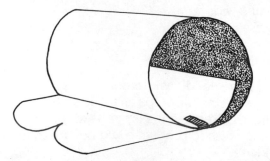

3 To make the frog's eyes, cut two half circles on the front of the rolled paper and lift these up to make two flaps.
4 You can then use the felt tip pens to add details to the eyes and perhaps draw a nose.

A red indian head-dress

This is what you need:

- *1 strip of card, 50cm by 3cm.*
- *Sellotape.*
- *Felt tip pens or crayons.*
- *A sheet of card, 20cm by 30cm.*
- *Scissors.*

Help the child to:

1 Colour the strip of card with patterns or bands of colour.
2 Measure the child's head and sellotape the strip of card accordingly.
3 On the sheet of card, draw some simple feather shapes and colour them in with bands of colour. Cut the feathers out and stick them on to the inside brim of the head band.
4 Alternatively, autumn leaves make super feathers – or you could always go out and find the real thing.

Paper hats

This is what you need:

Hat 1
- *A paper plate.*
- *Felt tip pens or crayons.*
- *Sellotape.*
- *Elasticated thread.*

Hat 2
- *A large paper bag.*
- *Scissors.*
- *Felt tip pens or crayons.*

Hat 3
- *A strip of paper, 50cm by 12cm.*
- *Felt tip pens or crayons.*
- *Scissors.*
- *Sellotape.*

Help the child to:

1 Make Hat 1 by decorating the paper plate with patterns, pictures or bands of colour. Sellotape a length of elasticated thread to the underside of the plate hat and put it on.
2 Make Hat 2 by decorating the paper bag, cut along one side of the bag and open it out before putting it on. DO REMIND LITTLE ONES NEVER TO PUT PLASTIC BAGS ON THEIR HEADS!
3 Make Hat 3 by decorating the strip of paper with colour or by cutting a pattern along one edge. Check the size of the child's head and sellotape the hat accordingly.

Stained-glass windows

This is what you need:

- *A sheet of black paper, 25cm by 35cm.*
- *Scissors.*
- *A pencil.*
- *Glue and a glue brush.*
- *Coloured tissue paper.*

Help the child to:

1 Draw some simple shapes or a picture on to the black paper. Try not to get too close to the edge of the paper and don't draw the shapes too close together. Cut the shapes out, which will leave lots of holes.
2 Alternatively, very little ones could dispense with drawing altogether. They could make holes by tearing a few pieces out of the centre of the paper.
3 Lay the black paper on to a covered table top and stick the coloured tissue over the holes.
4 When it is dry you can hang the picture on a window where the light will shine through the tissue.

It's always nice to visit a local church before making this picture so that children can see for themselves the beauty of stained glass.

Newspaper tree

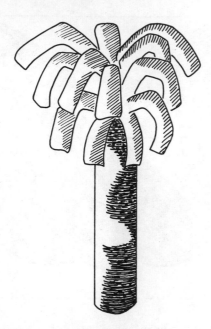

This is what you need:

- *1 old newspaper for each tree. (Preferably not tabloid.)*
- *Sellotape.*
- *Sharp scissors.*

Help the child to:

1 Lay the newspaper on the floor and open it out. Take the top four sheets of paper and lift them off the bottom sheets. Put them down again half on and half off the newspaper on the floor, so that they overlap.

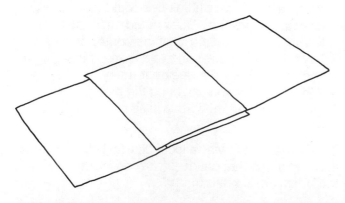

2 Now roll the newspaper up to make a tube and sellotape it into position.
3 Using the scissors cut two or three long slits in one end of the tube. The slits need to go at least half way down the length of the tube.

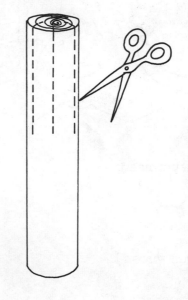

4 Put your fingers inside the tube at the cut end, take hold of the inside leaves of newspaper and gently pull upwards. A tree will rise up from the tube, looking remarkably like a palm tree.

Shiny paper collage

This is what you need:

- *1 sheet of paper.*
- *Glue and a glue brush.*
- *Scissors.*
- *As large a collection of shiny items as possible. For example, toffee paper, milk bottle tops, glitter, tinfoil, tinsel, and shiny wrapping paper.*

Help the child to:

Glue as many different shiny things as possible on to the paper. It really isn't necessary to create a "picture of something" as the quality of shininess is enough on its own.

Newspaper dolls

This is what you need:

- *Old newspapers.*
- *Sellotape.*
- *Scraps of material.*
- *A circle of white paper. If you draw round the top of a coffee cup the circle will be the right size.*
- *Felt tip pens or crayons.*

Help the child to:

1 Separate the sheets of newspaper and roll three sheets up to make three long tubes. Stick sellotape round the tubes to hold them in shape.
2 Take the first tube and make a loop by folding it in half and sticking the two ends together with sellotape. This forms the doll's body.

3 Take the second tube and thread it through the bottom of the loop made by the first tube. The second tube should hang down equally on both sides to form two legs. To prevent the legs from sliding out of the loop, tightly sellotape the legs together at the top.

4 To make the arms, push the third tube through the top of the loop, making sure that it sticks out equally on both sides, and sellotape it into position. If the arms seem a little too long, trim them with scissors.

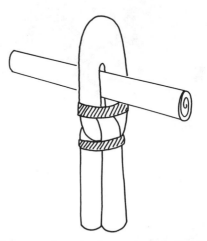

5 Draw a face on the circle and stick it with a piece of sellotape into position on the doll. Clothes can be added by simply wrapping a scrap of material round the body. Children seem to adore these dolls. They often mean far more to them than the shop-bought variety.

Shapes' collage

This is what you need:

- *Old colourful magazines.*
- *Scissors.*
- *Glue and a glue brush.*
- *A sheet of paper.*

Help the child to:

1 Decide on a simple shape like a square or a circle.
2 Look through the old magazines and see if you can find your shape in any of the pictures. For example, clocks and wheels are circles.
3 Cut out as many of the shapes as you can find and stick them on to the paper.

Faces' collage

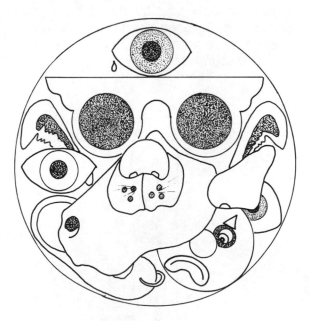

This is what you need:

- *Lots of old coloured magazines.*
- *Scissors.*
- *Glue and a glue brush.*
- *Sheets of paper.*
- *A felt tip pen.*

Help the child to:

1 Look for large colour photographs of people in the magazines and then cut out as many eyes, noses, ears and mouths as possible.
2 Draw a large circle on to the paper.
3 Make a face in the circle using the cut out features and glue them into position. You could also create fantastic monsters and giants with eight eyes, seven noses etc. Which one looks most like daddy?

Pasta collage

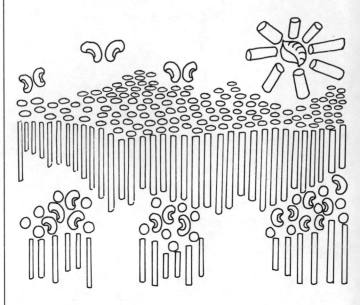

This is what you need:

- *Strong glue and a glue brush.*
- *A sheet of paper.*
- *As many different pasta shapes as possible (and you could also include rice and dried beans – though not, of course, red kidney beans).*
- *Felt tip pens or crayons.*

Help the child to:

1 Draw a simple picture on to the sheet of paper, or you could leave it plain.
2 Stick the pasta on to the picture or create patterns with all the different shapes.

Colour collage

This is what you need:

- *Old colourful magazines.*
- *Scissors.*
- *Glue and a glue brush.*
- *Scraps of material and wrapping paper of the right colour.*

Help the child to:

1 Decide on a colour, e.g. blue.
2 Look through the old magazines and find pictures of blue things, such as a blue dress and a blue car. Cut out as many blue pictures as possible and stick them, along with any scraps of blue material you might have, on to the paper.
3 Look round the house. What else is blue? Make a collection of blue objects and create a "blue" table where blue things can be displayed. This is an ideal way for little ones to learn their colours.

Draw round yourself

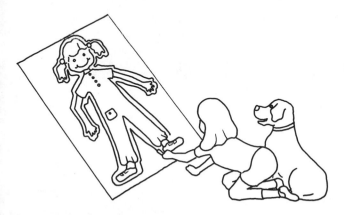

This is what you need:

- *1 thick black felt tip pen.*
- *1 roll of wallpaper lining paper. Or use the white side of an old roll of wallpaper.*
- *Felt tip pens or crayons.*
- *Scissors.*
- *Sellotape.*

Help the child to:

1 Lie down on a double sheet of paper, (Sellotape two sheets of paper side by side) and carefully draw round the child's outline with a felt tip pen.
2 Stand up again and, using crayons or paints, add all the little details to the outline e.g. a nose, hair, eyes, mouth and clothes.
3 When it is dry, why not cut the picture out and hang it on the child's bedroom door? Then everyone will know whose room it is – and who to blame for the mess inside.

Paper plate face

This is what you need:

- *1 paper plate.*
- *Felt tip pens or crayons.*
- *Glue and a glue brush.*
- *Scissors.*
- *Scraps of wool, material, coloured paper, milk bottle tops etc.*

Help the child to:

Create a face on the plate by using as many different mediums as possible. Wool makes great hair, a milk bottle top a nose, two buttons for eyes and so on.

Masks

This is what you need:

Mask 1
- A large paper bag.
- Felt tip pens, crayons or paints.
- Scissors.

Mask 2
- A piece of card, 30cm by 21cm.
- Elasticated thread.
- Scissors.
- Sellotape.
- Felt tip pens.
- Glue and a glue brush.
- Milk bottle tops, wool, scraps of material.

Help the child to:

1 Make Mask 1 by drawing or painting a face on to the paper bag and cutting out two holes for eyes. However, do remind little ones that it is not safe to put PLASTIC bags on heads!
2 It is perhaps safer to make Mask 2 by cutting out a simple mask shape, either full face or half face from a piece of card. Cut out two eye holes and decorate the mask before attaching the elasticated thread. The decoration can be really exciting for young children; for example, make a robot mask by sticking on lots of milk bottle tops.

A teddy bear plate

This is what you need:

- 1 paper plate.
- 5 brass paper fasteners.
- 1 sheet of coloured paper, 40cm by 20cm. A teddy bear colour would be nice i.e. brown or orange.
- Felt tip pens or crayons.
- Scissors.

Help the child to:

1 Draw a very simple teddy bear's head and four legs on to the coloured paper.

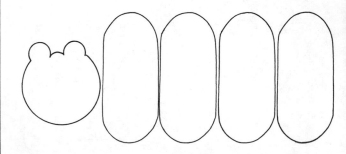

2 Cut the head and legs out and draw a face on the head and perhaps some buttons on the teddy bear's body, i.e. the paper plate.
3 Attach the head and legs on the paper plate body with the paper fasteners. Teddy can of course move his arms and legs, so why not get out the dolls' tea set and have a teddy bears' picnic. Daddy bear can do the washing-up.

Paper birds

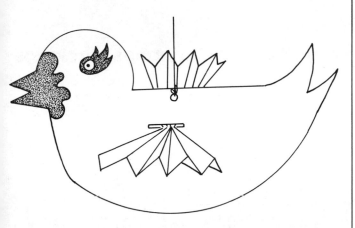

This is what you need:

- *1 piece of card, 20cm by 20cm.*
- *Elasticated thread.*
- *Scissors.*
- *Crayons or felt tip pens.*
- *A piece of pretty wrapping paper, 20cm by 20cm.*

Help the child to:

1 Draw a simple bird shape on to the piece of card and cut it out.
2 Draw an eye on both sides of the bird and colour in the beak.
3 With the scissors make a 3cm slit through the middle of the bird.

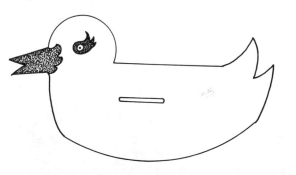

4 Fold the pretty paper as you would a fan and slot this through the slit in the bird. Gently pull the folded paper open so that it looks like the bird's wings. Attach a length of elastic to the back of the bird and watch it fly!

Paper bag puppet

This is what you need:

- *Old paper bags, one for each puppet.*
- *Old newspapers.*
- *Rubber bands.*
- *Felt tip pens or crayons.*
- *Long cardboard tubes (for example the centre from a roll of tinfoil), one for each puppet.*

Help the child to:

1 Draw a face on to the paper bag with the felt tip pens.
2 Stuff the bag with newspaper until it is nearly full.
3 Push the tube into the bag as far as it will go and fasten the bag to the tube with an elastic band. If you make enough of these puppets you can put on a play.

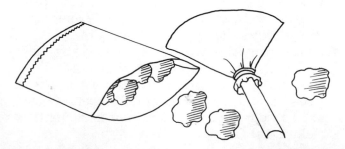

Just for Christmas

Paper doily snowflakes

This is what you need:

- White paint.
- A paint brush.
- A paper doily.
- A few sheets of coloured paper. The paper should be slightly larger than the doily.
- An old newspaper.

Help the child to:

1 Prepare a table top to work on by covering it with newspaper.
2 Place a doily on top of a sheet of coloured paper and use a brush to carefully dab white paint through all the tiny holes in the doily.
3 When all the holes have been covered with paint, peel the doily away from the paper. Underneath you will see a pretty snowflake pattern.
4 A very impressive picture can be made by cutting out lots of these snowflakes, dabbing them with glue and silver glitter, and arranging them on a large sheet of coloured paper. Alternatively, stick them on to windows, or hang them in groups to make a mobile.

A garland of Christmas stockings

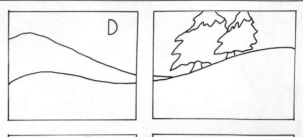
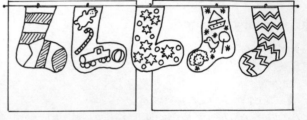

This is what you need:

- A long length of string or ribbon.
- Felt tip pens or paints.
- Several sheets of plain white paper.
- Glue and a glue brush.
- Scissors.
- Old catalogues or magazines with pictures of toys inside.
- Paper clips.

Help the child to:

1 Take the white paper and draw and cut out as many simple stocking shapes as possible. Each stocking needs to be about 20cm long. It might be easier if you make a template of a stocking shape out of thick card and draw round this.
2 Decorate the stockings. Paint some, and cut out pictures of toys from the catalogues to stick on to the rest.
3 Decide where you want to hang the stockings. Put the string or ribbon in position and fasten the stockings to it with the paper clips.

A snowstorm

This is what you need:

- *1 empty screw top jar with lid.*
- *2 tablespoons of waterproof filler.*
- *Plastic Christmas cake decorations, such as a robin or Father Christmas.*
- *A small piece of tinfoil.*

Help the child to:

1 Mix up the filler and put it in the bottom of the jar. Wipe away any filler that clings to the side of the jar – or the snowstorm will be hidden.
2 While the filler is still wet put the Christmas decoration in position and allow the filler to dry completely.

3 Fill the jar with cold water and tiny pieces of screwed-up tinfoil; these will form the snow. Screw the lid back on to the jar.
4 Shake well and put up your umbrella!

Santa

This is what you need:

- *1 toilet roll tube.*
- *Cotton wool.*
- *Sellotape.*
- *Red crepe paper, cut into a strip 18cm by 22cm.*
- *A black felt tip pen.*
- *2 small sheets of sticky-backed paper, black and pink.*
- *Scissors.*
- *Glue and a glue brush.*

Help the child to:

1 Roll the red crepe paper round the tube and fasten it into position with a little piece of sellotape. Then tuck the loose ends of the paper inside the tube.
2 Cut the black paper into a strip 1cm by 15cm and stick this round the middle of the tube. This will form Santa's belt.
3 Cut a circle from the pink paper, about the size of a 10p coin, and draw a happy face on it before sticking it into position on the tube.
4 Take some tiny pieces of cotton wool and glue these round Santa's face to form hair and a beard. Santa could be a container for a small Christmas gift such as a chocolate bar.

Frosty hands Christmas cards

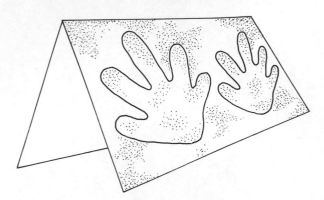

This is what you need:

- *A shallow container.*
- *White handprint paint – see the recipe in the 'Paint and Crayons' section.*
- *A piece of coloured card 22cm by 30cm. Dark colours such as purple or blue look best.*
- *Silver glitter.*
- *Glue and a glue brush.*
- *A pencil.*

Help the child to:

1 Fold the card in half, so that the front of the card is about 15cm by 22cm, and write a Christmas message inside. If the child is too young to copy a message from a piece of paper, or copy underneath your writing, try writing a dotted message and ask him or her to join the dots together. Do make sure that the child forms the letters correctly e.g. starting at the top of the h, and use lower-case letters rather than capitals.

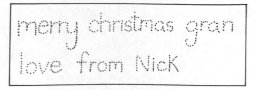

2 Dip both hands into the paint and press them side by side on to the front of the card. Children really enjoy hand printing, so while the card is drying, let them continue to hand print on to old newspaper.

3 When the card is dry, let the child dab some glue on to the handprints and then sprinkle the glue with silver glitter.

Grans always seem delighted to receive a card with "little hands" on.

An angel

This is what you need:

- *1 toilet roll tube.*
- *Tinfoil approx 18cm by 18cm.*
- *Glue and a glue brush.*
- *1 paper doily – either white or silver.*
- *A piece of white paper approx 6cm by 6cm.*
- *Scissors.*
- *A felt tip pen.*
- *Sellotape.*

Help the child to:

1 Wrap the tinfoil tightly round the tube and sellotape it into position. Tuck the loose ends of the tinfoil into the top and bottom of the tube.
2 Glue the doily into position behind the tube. If you find the doily is too big, cut it in half.
3 Cut out a circle from the white paper. Draw a pretty face on the circle with the felt tip pen.
4 Glue the face on to the toilet roll.
5 You could hang a group of these angels together in a corner of the room to make a very attractive Christmas mobile.

Snowman

This is what you need:

- *3 sheets of black paper: one 10cm by 10cm.*
  one 5cm by 10cm.
  one 2cm by 10cm.
- *A toilet roll tube.*
- *Cotton wool.*
- *Glue and a glue brush.*
- *A tiny piece of red paper.*
- *A small straight twig about 15cm long.*
- *Scissors.*

Help the child to:

1 Cut two small holes on opposite sides of the tube, about 3cm from one end. Then push the twig through the holes, so that it sticks out equally on each side. This will form the Snowman's arms.

2 Using the glue and the cotton wool, cover the tube with "snow".
3 Take the 5cm by 10cm piece of black paper and cut out six tiny circles. Stick these into position, using two for eyes, one for a nose and three as buttons.
4 Cut out a small mouth from the red paper and stick it on to the Snowman.
5 Now to make his hat. Take the 10cm by 10cm piece of black paper, cut out a circle, slightly larger than the top of the Snowman's body, and stick this on top of the Snowman. Make a tube shape with the 2cm by 10cm piece of black paper and stick this on top of the black paper circle.

A Postman Pat Box

This is what you need:

- *A large empty grocery box.*
- *Lots of red paint and a paint brush.*
- *Sharp scissors.*
- *A pencil and some crayons.*
- *Old envelopes and a few new ones.*
- *Old Christmas and birthday cards.*
- *An old pillowcase.*

Help the child to:

1 Cut a "letter box" hole in the side of the grocery box.
2 Paint all over the outside of the box with the red paint.
3 When the paint has dried your Postman Pat Box is ready. Children can now have great fun posting their cards and pretending to be Postman Pat. The new envelopes can have "pretend" writing on the front and "pretend" stamps can be drawn on them too.
Use the pillowcase as a mail sack and if there is only one child involved, why not put a doll or teddy in each room so that Postman Pat has plenty of people to deliver letters to.

It's certainly quicker than the first-class post.

Christmas tree decorations

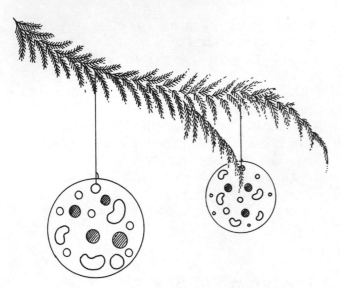

This is what you need:

- Dry lentils, peas, beans and rice. (Don't use red kidney beans.)
- A piece of card 20cm by 20cm.
- Scissors.
- Strong glue and a glue brush.
- Gold or silver spray.
- A felt tip pen or pencil.
- Small shapes to draw round, such as a jam jar lid.
- Ribbon or strong thread.

Help the child to:

1 Put the jam jar lid on to the piece of card and draw round it to make a circle. If the card is large enough you should be able to make several circles.
2 Cut the shapes out and make a small hole near the edge of each one with the scissors.
3 Cover the shapes with glue and while the glue is still wet stick the dried peas etc into position. Try to avoid covering the hole near the edge of each shape.
4 When dry the decorations can be sprayed silver or gold. To hang them on to the Christmas tree, you simply thread a loop of ribbon through the hole.

Christmas tree

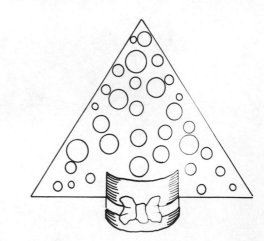

This is what you need:

- A toilet roll tube.
- A piece of card, 14cm by 16cm.
- Scissors.
- A pencil or felt tip pen.
- Glue and a glue brush.
- Glitter – 2 or 3 different colours would be nice.
- Green paint.
- Red paint.
- 2 paint brushes.
- 30cm of red, gold or green ribbon.

Help the child to:

1 Cut off a 6cm long piece from one end of the toilet roll tube. This will make a tub for the tree to stand on. Make two slits on opposite sides of the tub. The slits need to be about 3cm deep. Paint the tub red.
2 Draw and cut out a very simple fir tree shape from the piece of card. Then paint both sides of the tree green.
3 When the tree has dried, dab tiny spots of glue all over one side and immediately sprinkle these with glitter. Wait for the first side to dry and then repeat the process on the other side.
4 Slot the tree through the slits in the red painted tub. Then tie a bow of ribbon around the bottom of the tub. The Christmas tree could easily be made into a hanging decoration by threading a loop of ribbon through a hole made in the top of the tree.

A snowman picture

This is what you need:

- *2 sheets of black paper: one 30cm by 25cm.*
  one 10cm by 10cm.
- *Glue and a glue brush.*
- *Cotton wool.*
- *A piece of bright material about 10cm by 10cm.*
- *A sheet of colourful paper 12cm by 12cm.*
- *White chalk.*
- *Scissors.*

Help the child to:

1 Use the chalk to draw a very simple snowman outline on the large sheet of black paper. Add some falling snow and a snowy patch at the bottom of the paper for Mr Snowman to stand on.

2 Spread glue all over the snowman shape and cover him with cotton wool snowballs.
3 Cut out six circles from the small piece of black paper. Stick these into position, using two for eyes, one for a nose, and three as buttons.
4 Make the snowman's scarf by cutting out two small strips from the material and sticking them into position. Finally, cut out a very simple hat shape from the sheet of coloured paper, and stick this on to Mr Snowman's head.

Cooking

Biscuit faces

This is what you need:

- *A round plain biscuit, for example a digestive.*
- *2 teaspoons of cream cheese.*
- *2 teaspoons of margarine or butter.*
- *2 raisins.*
- *1 thin slice of carrot.*
- *1 thin slice of cucumber cut in half.*
- *Cress.*
- *A knife for spreading.*
- *A bowl for mixing.*

Help the child to:

1 Cream together the cream cheese and margarine.
2 Spread the cheese mixture on to the biscuit. Be sure to spread the mixture to the edge of the biscuit. This is quite straightforward; the trick is to avoid spreading it on to the surrounding floor, ceiling or sibling. This takes practice.
3 Arrange the fruit and vegetables to form a face. This is your chance to persuade the child that a thin slice of carrot, some cucumber and some cream cheese really does look like daddy.

Party biscuits

This is what you need:

- *Plain digestive biscuits.*
- *Icing sugar.*
- *Different food colourings.*
- *A jug of hot water.*
- *A bowl for mixing.*
- *A dessertspoon.*
- *A teaspoon.*
- *A quantity of small sweets, sugar strands, coloured balls, glace cherries etc.*
- *A flat baking tray or wire cooling rack.*
- *A knife.*

Help the child to:

1 Put a heaped dessertspoon of icing sugar in a bowl and add hot water a little at a time until the mixture is smooth but not too runny. You may like to add some food colouring.
2 Using a teaspoon spread a little of the icing sugar mixture over the top of a digestive biscuit. The icing needs to be quite thickly spread or the sweet decorations will drop off.
3 Decorate the iced biscuit with sweets and chopped cherries.
4 Place the finished biscuits on the tray or rack to harden.

Catherine wheels

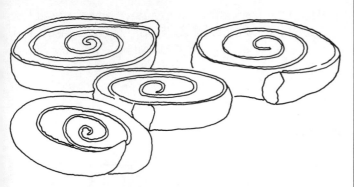

This is what you need:

- *1 packet of frozen puff pastry – thawed.*
- *1 jar of marmite.*
- *A blunt knife.*
- *A small quantity of flour.*
- *A rolling pin.*
- *A flat baking tray.*
- *A cooling rack.*

Help the child to:

1 Roll out the pastry thinly on a floured surface.
2 With a blunt knife, cut the pastry to make a rectangular shape, about 30cm by 20cm. Cut the rectangle into strips 4cm wide and then cut each strip in half.

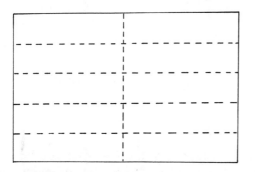

3 Use the knife to spread the marmite quite thinly over the top of each strip of pastry and then roll each strip up like a swiss roll.
4 Place the rolls of pastry on a baking tray and cook in the oven (gas mark 4, 180 degrees) for 20 minutes.

Bird cake

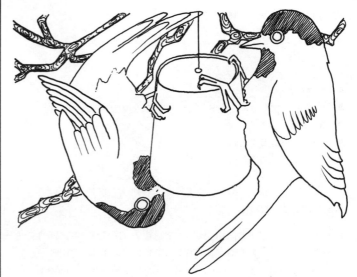

This is what you need:

- *1 empty yogurt pot.*
- *A piece of string about 45cm long.*
- *A sharp pair of scissors – for a grown-up.*
- *4oz of cheap lard.*
- *A saucepan.*
- *A large bowl.*
- *A dessertspoon.*
- *A selection from the following: breadcrumbs, chopped bacon rind, chopped apple, currants, cake or biscuit crumbs, peanuts.*

Help the child to:

1 Make a large knot on the end of the piece of string. Make a small hole in the bottom of the yogurt pot and thread the string through until the knot is inside the pot.
2 Put your breadcrumbs etc into the bowl.
3 Gently melt the lard in the saucepan and then pour it on to the ingredients in the bowl. (An adult should pour hot fat.)
4 Stir the mixture thoroughly until everything is well coated with fat and then spoon it into the prepared yogurt pot. Press the mixture down quite firmly.
5 Wait until the cake has set before taking it into the garden to hang up for the birds.

Fresh juice

This is what you need:

- *An orange or lemon – 1 piece of fruit per two children.*
- *A lemon squeezer.*
- *2oz sugar.*
- *Half a pint of water in a small saucepan.*
- *A jug.*
- *A dessertspoon.*
- *A sharp knife – for a grown-up.*
- *A sieve.*

Help the child to:

1 Put the sugar in the saucepan with the water and gently bring it to the boil, stirring all the time. (Obviously an adult had better do this.) Leave the sugar water in the pan to cool.
2 Cut the fruit in half and take the juice out with the lemon squeezer.
3 Sieve the juice into the jug and add the sugar water, stir well, chill and drink. Afterwards why not grow a little lemon tree by planting the pips in an empty yogurt pot filled with soil?

Individual buns

This is what you need:

- *A bowl. (Empty margarine or large ice-cream tubs make super bowls for young children to use.)*
- *A teaspoon.*
- *A tablespoon.*
- *Some paper cake cases.*
- *A baking tray.*

Each child takes:

- *1 tablespoon of SR flour.*
- *1 teaspoon of soft margarine.*
- *1 teaspoon of sugar.*
- *2 teaspoons of currants.*
- *2 tablespoons of milk/egg mixture. (2 eggs + 1 pint of milk)*

Help the child to:

1 Put all the ingredients into a bowl and stir well.
2 Spoon the mixture into a couple of cake cases and place on a baking tray. Cook in the oven for 10 minutes (gas mark 6 or 200 degrees).

Soup

This is what you need:

- *As many different vegetables as possible.*
- *A blunt knife.*
- *A sharp knife – for a grown-up.*
- *A large saucepan.*
- *Cold water.*
- *Salt.*
- *This makes a "souper" group activity for a cold winter's day so, if the soup is being made at playgroup, you will also need empty yogurt pots (1 for each child) and cling film.*

Help the child to:

1 Peel, trim and cut up the vegetables into small pieces. Potatoes are the easiest for small hands.
2 Wash the chunks of vegetables and then put them all in the saucepan.
3 Pour some water into the saucepan, add a little salt and then set it to simmer on the stove until cooked. If making this at playgroup, each child can take home a yogurt pot of soup covered with cling film.

Chocolate fruit

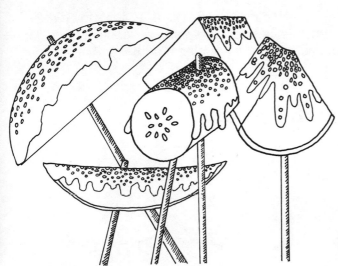

This is what you need:

- *A selection of fruit, such as an apple, a pear and a banana.*
- *A blunt knife.*
- *Cocktail sticks.*
- *1 bar of cooking chocolate.*
- *A double boiler or a small saucepan.*
- *Sugar strands or similar tiny sweets.*
- *A plate.*
- *A saucer.*
- *A wire cooling rack.*

Help the child to:

1 Cut the fruit up into chunks and spear each piece with a cocktail stick.
2 Put the tiny sweets on the saucer.
3 Melt the chocolate in the double boiler or saucepan and bring it to the table. Obviously an adult had better do this.
4 While an adult holds the saucepan steady the child can dip each piece of fruit into the chocolate and then either dip the fruit into the sweets or sprinkle a few sweets on to the chocolate fruit.
5 Place the fruit on a wire rack to set. Meanwhile, the washing-up can be tackled by willing helpers using tongues and fingers. Washing up the washers-up may take longer.

Marzipan animals

This is what you need:

- *1 packet of ready prepared marzipan. (If you can't obtain marzipan then make a substitute by creaming together 2oz castor sugar, 2oz block margarine, 8oz cake crumbs and a few drops of almond essence.)*
- *Edible silver balls.*
- *Currants.*
- *Almonds.*
- *Pieces of clean string.*
- *A small amount of flour.*

Help the child to:

1 Take a small lump of marzipan (about the size of a tangerine) and on a lightly floured surface, mould the marzipan to form a ball.
2 Turn the ball of marzipan into a mouse by adding two almonds for ears, two currants for eyes, a silver ball for a nose and a length of string for a tail.
3 Or make a hedgehog by using almonds as the hedgehog's quills, two currants for eyes and a silver ball for a nose.

Of course the children will probably have their own suggestions for animals they would like to make. You need quite a lot of marzipan to make a dinosaur.

Frosted fruit

This is what you need:

- *Some castor sugar on a saucer.*
- *1 egg.*
- *A selection of washed fruit. (Black grapes, red apples and green pears look most effective.)*
- *Cocktail sticks.*
- *A blunt knife.*
- *A small bowl.*
- *A fork.*
- *A wire cooling rack.*

Help the child to:

1 Separate the egg white from the yolk, and put the white of egg into the bowl.
2 Whisk the egg white up with the fork.
3 Cut the fruit up into bite-sized chunks and spear each piece with a cocktail stick.
4 Dip the fruit first into the egg white and then into the castor sugar.
5 Place the fruit on the cooling rack to dry and harden. Frosted fruit makes a very pretty present especially if put in a home-made paper basket.

Edible animals

This is what you need:

- *Cocktail sticks.*
- *Chunks of fresh fruit or raw vegetables.*
- *Chunks of cold cooked sausage or cheese.*

Help the child to:

Arrange the food on the cocktail sticks to create monsters, pets, or wild animals – and eat them! These animals are very popular at parties.

Pastry people

This is what you need:

- *8oz of readymade shortcrust pastry.*
- *Currants or raisins.*
- *Glacé cherries.*
- *A little flour.*
- *A teaspoon of margarine.*
- *A flat baking tray.*

Help the child to:

1 Grease the baking tray with the margarine.
2 Lightly flour a working surface and divide the pastry into 6 pieces. Roll two of the pieces into balls (these will form the head and body), and make sausage shapes with the other four pieces (these will form the arms and legs).
3 Lay the different parts of the body into position on the baking tray and join the pastry by gently pinching the different parts together.
4 Add a face, buttons, shoes, fingers etc by pressing the fruit into the pastry. Glaze with a little beaten egg for a really professional finish. then cook for 20 minutes in the oven, gas mark 4, 180 degrees.

Chocolate nests

This is what you need:

- *A double boiler or small saucepan.*
- *A mixing bowl.*
- *1 dessertspoon.*
- *1 teaspoon.*
- *Paper cake cases.*
- *A wire cooling rack.*
- *A large block of cooking chocolate.*
- *2oz of margarine.*
- *2 tablespoons of golden syrup.*
- *Rice crispies or cornflakes.*
- *Small chocolate or sugar eggs.*

Help the child to:

1 Gently heat the chocolate, margarine and syrup in the saucepan until all the ingredients have melted together. An adult had better do this.
2 Sprinkle a generous amount of rice crispies into a bowl. An adult can now pour the melted chocolate mixture into the bowl and the child can stir the contents together.
3 With a teaspoon fill each paper case with the chocolate/crispies mixture. Try to make them look like nests by forming a slight hollow in the centre.
4 Put the nests on to the cooling rack and fill each one with little eggs. If you are giving some of the nests as Easter presents, then put a tiny yellow chick on top. Make the chick from a yellow cotton wool ball, (multi-coloured cotton wool balls are usually obtainable from the chemist) and add eyes and a beak with a felt tip pen.

Cook a real fish

This is what you need:

- *1 whole fresh mackerel or herring.*
- *A little butter.*
- *A sharp knife – for a grown-up.*

1 This really is the age of the "fish finger". Many children have never seen a fresh fish prepared and cooked, yet they do find it fascinating. The mackerel is a good fish to choose as it's large enough for the children to handle easily and it is an extremely beautiful fish.

Allow plenty of time to look at and talk about the fish. Can the children see it's gills, eyes, fins, tongue and teeth?

2 To prepare the fish, you cut off the head and tail, slit along the belly and remove all the intestines, then lay it cut side down on the table and press firmly along the backbone until the fish is flattened. Turn the fish over and carefully pull out the backbone.

Children are usually full of questions during the preparation, so perhaps you had better read up a little fish anatomy before you start!

3 Rinse the fish under the cold water tap and then grill with a little butter on top.

Group pictures

Baa Baa Black Sheep

This is what you need:

- *1 large sheet of paper.*
- *1 jar of thick green paint.*
- *2 or 3 paint brushes.*
- *Lots of black tissue paper.*
- *Glue and glue brushes.*
- *A thick black felt tip pen.*

Help the children to:

1 Draw the very simple outline of a sheep on the paper.
2 Taking turns, use the green paint to surround the sheep with grass. While the painting is going on, ask the remaining children to rip the tissue paper into small pieces about 10cm by 10cm, and then to crush the tissue up into balls.
3 When the green paint is dry, stick the tissue balls close together on the sheep.
4 This picture could be made more elaborate by the addition of three paper bags with some black wool in and three painted figures. Paint the figures, a man, a woman and a little boy, on separate sheets of paper before cutting them out and sticking them on to the main picture.

A patchwork collage

This is what you need:

- *Strong glue and glue brushes.*
- *Thin card cut into patchwork shapes, for example squares or hexagons. A good size for a square would be 20cm by 20cm.*
- *A collection of things with as many textures as possible. Sand, rice, macaroni, wood shavings, scraps of shiny paper, wool, material, and shells would be excellent.*
- *A very large sheet of paper.*

Help the children to:

1 Cover one side of the card shape with glue and stick just one of the textures to it. Produce as many different cards as possible.
2 When the card shapes are dry, arrange them on a sheet of paper in patchwork fashion. When you are all pleased with the effect, glue the shapes into position. Of course, do make sure it is only shapes you are glueing into position, tempting as it may be. . . .

Eggbox dragon

This is what you need:

- *A very large sheet of paper.*
- *Lots of empty cardboard eggboxes.*
- *Scissors for the children.*
- *Several jars of thick green paint.*
- *Paint brushes.*
- *1 jar of thick red paint.*
- *1 thick black felt tip pen.*
- *Strong glue and glue brushes.*

Help the children to:

1 Cut the lids off the eggboxes.
2 Paint the bottom half of the eggboxes green. Only the outside of the eggbox really needs to be painted, but little ones often like to paint them all over.
3 At one end of the big sheet of paper, draw a very simple dragon's head. You don't need to draw a body.
4 Paint the head green and paint some red fire coming from the dragon's mouth.
5 When both the egg boxes and the dragon's head are dry, you can start to stick the egg boxes into position. Don't worry too much about where they go but try to put them close together. When the dragon has been "built" you could use the felt tip pen to add some simple wings.

Big red bus

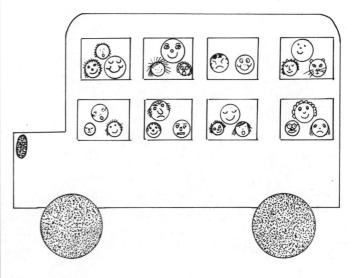

This is what you need:

- *A large sheet of paper.*
- *A large jar of thick red paint.*
- *Several paint brushes.*
- *A large jar of thick black paint.*
- *Aprons.*
- *Small paper plates, or you could cut out circles from white paper.*
- *Felt tip pens or crayons.*
- *Glue and glue brushes.*
- *A thick black felt tip pen.*

Help the children to:

1 Use the thick felt tip pen to draw the outline of a double-decker bus on the large sheet of paper.
2 Let the children take turns to paint the big bus "red" and the wheels "black". Don't forget to remind them NOT to paint the windows on the bus.
3 Meanwhile, those waiting to paint can be making a "face" out of the paper plate or circle of white paper. A simple face can be drawn with crayons or a more elaborate "face" could have wool hair added.
4 When the bus is dry, stick the faces into position at the windows. You could then sing that all time playgroup favourite "The wheels on the bus go round and round".

A free-for-all wall

This is what you need:

For day 1
- *A suitable wall, where a long roll of paper can be pinned or stuck.*
- *A roll of wall-lining paper.*
- *Lots of different coloured paints.*
- *Lots of paint brushes.*
- *Aprons.*
- *Newspaper for the floor.*
- *Bowls of water for washing hands.*

For day 2
- *Lots of pots of glue.*
- *Glue brushes.*
- *Lots of old magazines, catalogues etc.*
- *Anything at all that might be interesting to stick on the wall – such as scraps of material and wool, milk-bottle tops, wood shavings etc.*
- *Lots of scissors.*
- *Aprons.*
- *Newspapers for the floor.*
- *Bowls of water for washing hands.*

Help the children to:

1 Pin the paper to the wall, cover the floor with newspaper and put aprons on.
2 On day 1, put the paints and brushes on a table near to the paper and ask the children to paint! Some children might want to hand print but do remind them not to paint each other.

3 On day 2, let the cutting and sticking commence. Encourage the children to find interesting objects, and pictures from the magazines and stick them on to the painted picture. The result of all this effort will probably be snapped up by the Tate gallery.

Eggshell Humpty Dumpty

This is what you need:

- *A collection of washed eggshells.*
- *A large sheet of paper.*
- *A thick black felt tip pen.*
- *A large jar of thick red paint.*
- *2 or 3 paint brushes.*
- *Strong glue.*
- *Glue brushes.*

Help the children to:

1 Use the felt tip pen to draw a simple brick wall on the bottom half of the paper. Try to draw at least as many bricks as there are children.
2 Ask each child in turn to paint a brick in the wall with the red paint.
3 When the paint is dry draw a large egg shape with a face on it, sitting on top of the wall.
4 Crush the egg shells, not too finely, and stick them all over Humpty Dumpty. Obviously now would be a good time to sing the nursery rhyme.

A giant totem-pole

This is what you need:

- *Lots of empty cardboard grocery boxes.*
- *Large pots of different coloured paints.*
- *Lots of paint brushes.*
- *Aprons.*
- *Newspaper for the floor.*
- *Strong glue and glue brushes or double-sided sticky tape.*

Help the children to:

1 Cover a large area of the floor with newspaper, or if it's a warm sunny day, move outside. Put the aprons on the children, give them the paint and ask them to decorate the boxes.
2 When the boxes have dried sufficiently, stick them one on top of the other until all the boxes have been used up.
3 It's now time to dance round the totem-pole. Why not have some musical instruments such as bells and tambourines ready, or perhaps a tape of suitably happy music. And don't forget the cotton wool for your ears.

A handprint lion

This is what you need:

- *1 large sheet of paper. Several stuck together would do.*
- *1 thick black felt tip pen.*
- *3 bowls of thick hand paint. (You can find the recipe in the Paint and Crayons section.) Since we are making a lion, I would suggest lion type colours, for example brown, orange and yellow. More exotic lions are of course possible.*

Help the children to:

1 Draw an outline of a lion's head on to the paper.
2 Ask the children to take turns to print their hands round the lion's head. It doesn't matter if the hands overlap on the paper. But try to keep them on the paper and off the by-standers (easier said than done!). The prints form the lion's mane.

Alternatively, the coward's way out is to make the hand prints on separate sheets of paper. Allow them to dry and cut them out before sticking them on to the lion. Even this way has plenty of scope for mess at the sticking stage, so you don't miss out on too much.

Daffodils

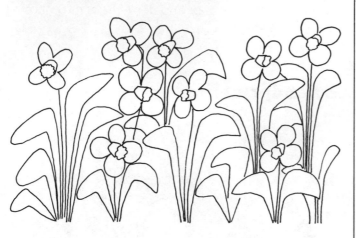

This is what you need:

- *Newspaper for the floor.*
- *A large sheet of paper.*
- *Lots of empty cardboard eggboxes.*
- *Scissors for the children.*
- *A few jars of thick yellow paint.*
- *A large jar of thick green paint.*
- *2 pieces of card for each child, 10cm by 10cm.*
- *Paint brushes.*
- *Strong glue.*
- *Glue brushes.*

Help the children to:

1 Lay the large sheet of paper on some newspaper on the floor. Ask the children a few at a time to paint some "green leaves" on to the paper.
2 While the painting is going on, the rest of the children can be cutting or ripping the cups from the egg boxes and painting them yellow.
3 Take the pieces of card and help the children to cut out a simple petal shape from each one. These are also painted yellow.

4 When all the paint is dry, the children can start sticking. To make a daffodil, stick an egg box cup, hollow side up, in the centre of each petal shape.

5 When the glue has dried, you can stick the daffodils into position on the green painted paper.

This picture takes time to produce, but the effect can be quite stunning, and if space won't permit a wall display, each child could make an individual "daffodil picture" to take home. A picture like this can easily be made into a lovely card for Mother's Day.

Fingerprint snowdrops

This is what you need:

- *A large sheet of paper.*
- *A big jar of thick green paint.*
- *Several paint brushes.*
- *A large quantity of white handprint paint – see the hand paint recipe in the 'Paint and crayons' section.*
- *A large shallow bowl or tray.*
- *Aprons.*
- *Newspaper for the floor.*
- *Bowls of water for washing hands.*

Help the children to:

1 Paint the large sheet of paper with "green leaves", making sure that as much of the paper as possible is covered.
2 When the leaves have dried, provide the white finger paint in the shallow bowl and ask the children to use finger tips only to print white snowdrops all over the green leaves. The result can be very pretty.

A blossom tree

This is what you need:

- A very large sheet of paper.
- A thick black felt tip pen.
- A big jar of thick brown paint.
- A big jar of thick green paint.
- 6 paint brushes.
- Newspaper for the floor.
- Lots of small lightweight twigs.
- Lots of tissue paper in pastel colours.
- Sellotape.
- Glue and glue brushes.
- 4 or 5 small potatoes cut in half.

Help the children to:

1 Use the black felt tip pen to draw a very simple tree trunk outline on to the large sheet of paper. Leave plenty of room at the top of the paper for twigs.

2 Stick the twigs into position with sellotape. If it has been impossible to find enough twigs of a suitable size, the children could draw some as well.

3 Small groups of children can now take turns to fill in the tree trunk with brown paint and use the potatoes to print green leaves amongst the twigs. Obviously it is easier for the children if the "tree" is on the floor while it is being made.

4 While the painting and printing is going on, ask the remaining children to make some blossom by ripping the tissue paper into small pieces (about 10cm by 10cm) and lightly crushing the tissue into balls.

5 When the tree has dried, ask each child to take a handful of tissue blossom and stick it amongst the twigs. You should now have a very pretty blossom tree inside your playgroup but if space doesn't allow for such a large item, each child could do a small, individual tree on paper.

Inspiration for a wet day

Pastry models

This is what you need:

- *1 large bowl.*
- *1 cup of salt.*
- *2 cups of plain flour.*
- *Water.*
- *Paints and varnish.*

Help the child to:

1 Mix together the salt and the flour in the bowl.
2 Add some water to this mixture a little at a time
  until you have formed a dough.
3 On a floury surface make the dough into models of
  animals or people. Or make pretend food such as
  sausages, cakes and peas. Model food can later be
  used to create a pretend shop.
4 Fire the models by placing them on a baking sheet
  in a very low oven for several hours. Remove them
  when they are completely dry and hard.
5 When the models are cold, paint them with poster
  paint. If you want to make them look really nice,
  you can finish them off with a coat of varnish.

Blowing bubbles

This is what you need:

- *A steep-sided basin or bowl.*
- *A little warm water.*
- *Washing up liquid.*
- *A straw.*

Help the child to:

1 Put a little warm water in the bottom of the basin
  and add a squirt of washing up liquid.
2 Give the child the straw and ask her to blow into
  the soapy water. Watch the bubbles! Do remind
  little ones to blow and not suck.

An inside sand-pit

This is what you need:

- *A washing-up bowl or cardboard box.*
- *A box of dry porridge oats, or dry lentils and rice.*
- *An assortment of spoons, cups, small jugs, bowls
  etc.*
- *An old newspaper.*

Help the child to:

1 Place the washing-up bowl on a sheet of
  newspaper on the kitchen floor.
2 Fill the bowl with the dry porridge oats.
3 Give the child the spoons, cups and other items to
  play with in the oats. Obviously you can't build a
  castle out of dry oats but this doesn't seem to
  matter. Little children love to fill and empty
  containers. This activity is also very suitable for a
  sick child confined to bed. Put the washing up
  bowl on a tray and be prepared to re-make the
  bed afterwards.

Shaving foam pictures

This is what you need:

- 1 spray can of shaving foam. (If you haven't got any shaving foam, you can make your own by whisking together soap flakes with a little warm water.)
- 1 smooth table top or tray.

Help the child to:

1 Put a generous squirt of foam on to the table top.
2 Now for the fun! Encourage the child to spread the foam all over the table with his hands.
3 Make pictures in the foam by using a finger to draw with. This looks especially good on dark surfaces. When finished with one picture or pattern the child can spread the foam and start again. It's amazing where it gets spread to – but it's very easy to clear up.

A recipe for play-dough

This is what you need:

- 3lb plain flour.
- 1lb salt.
- 2 tablespoons of cooking oil.
- Approx ¾ pint of warm water.
- Powder paint or food colouring.
- A large mixing bowl.
- A wooden spoon.

Help the child to:

1 Put the flour, salt, dry powder paint and oil into the mixing bowl.
2 Add the warm water a little at a time and mix well. When all the water has been added, knead the mixture for several minutes.
3 This play-dough will keep well for several weeks if kept in an air-tight container or a plastic bag.

Finger people

This is what you need:

- A felt tip pen.

Help the child to:

1 Draw a face with the felt tip pen on each of the child's fingers. Make some of the faces happy and others sad. Make some look like grown-ups and others like children.
2 Make up stories for the finger people or use them in finger rhymes such as:

"Mr Thumb, Mr Thumb, where are you?
Here I am, here I am. How do you do.
Peter pointer, Peter pointer, where are you?
Here I am, here I am. How do you do.
Mr Tall, Mr Tall, where are you?
Here I am, here I am. How do you do.
Ruby ring, Ruby ring, where are you?
Here I am, here I am. How do you do.
Baby small, baby small, where are you?
Here I am, here I am. How do you do."

Paint and crayons

Printing with plasticine

This is what you need:

- Old, unwanted plasticine.
- Sheets of paper.
- Different coloured paints.
- Paint brushes.
- A collection of small objects, capable of creating marks on plasticine, e.g. a cocktail stick, a comb, an acorn, a fork, dice.

Help the child to:

1 Soften the plasticine by working it with your fingers, and make several ping-pong sized balls with it.
2 Flatten one side of each ball slightly by pressing the ball on to a table top.

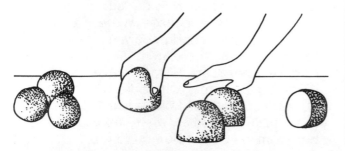

3 Take your collection of objects and use them to create patterns on the flattened side of the plasticine balls.

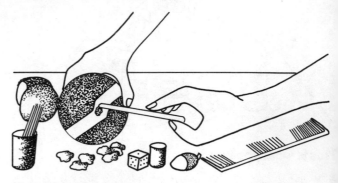

4 Use a paint brush and lightly paint over the patterned plasticine. Print the painted pattern on to the paper.

Rubbings

This is what you need:

- Sheets of white paper.
- Thick wax crayons of various colours, although black has perhaps the most dramatic effect.
- Blu-tack. (This is optional but it does help little ones to keep the paper steady.)

Help the child to:

1 Find objects with patterns on them either inside or outdoors : tree bark, coins, frosted glass, leaves, the manhole cover etc.
2 Ask the child to close her eyes for a moment. Can she feel the pattern with her fingers? If the answer is "yes", put a piece of paper on top of it. Hold the paper steady with hands or blu-tack and rub over the top of the paper with a wax crayon.

Why not have a competition to see how many different patterns you can find?

Bubbles on paper

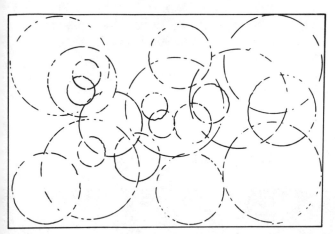

This is what you need:

- *An empty deep-sided margarine tub.*
- *1 drinking straw.*
- *1 tablespoon washing up liquid.*
- *4 tablespoons powder paint.*
- *1 cup of water.*
- *Sheets of paper.*

Help the child to:

1 Put the powder paint, washing up liquid and water into the margarine tub and mix well. The mixture needs to be fairly runny.
2 Using the drinking straw, blow bubbles in the paint mixture until the bubbles come well up over the rim of the margarine tub. To avoid children turning blue and the floor turning green, remind little ones to blow and not suck.

3 Quickly put the paper on top of the bubbles.

4 Remove the paper and you should see a bubble picture. To make it even more exciting for the children, use lots of different colours.

Fold-over butterflies

This is what you need:

- *Sheets of paper.*
- *Coloured paints.*
- *Paint brushes.*

Help the child to:

1 Fold a sheet of paper in half and then open it out again.
2 Dab blobs of different coloured paints on to one half of the paper.
3 Fold the paper again and press down firmly.
4 Unfold the paper to reveal a beautiful butterfly. This is a very popular activity, so have lots of paper ready.

Rainy day finger prints

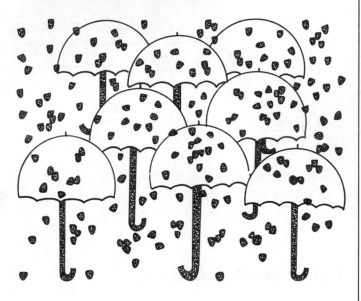

This is what you need:

- *1 sheet of white paper, a good size would be 25cm by 35cm.*
- *Several pieces of coloured paper, about 8cm by 16cm.*
- *1 black felt tip pen.*
- *Scissors.*
- *Glue and a glue brush.*
- *Blue paint.*

Help the child to:

1 Draw simple umbrella shapes on to the coloured paper and cut them out.

2 Arrange and glue the umbrellas on to the white paper. They look very pretty if they overlap slightly (which is very fortunate because they probably will!). Add the umbrella handles with the felt tip pen.
3 Dip the very tips of fingers into the blue paint and create finger tip raindrops all over the umbrellas.

Wax and paint

This is what you need:

- *A sheet of white paper.*
- *Wax crayons. Try to avoid very dark colours such as black, purple, dark blue and brown.*
- *Black paint, made as thin as possible.*
- *A paint brush.*

Help the child to:

1 Use the wax crayons to create a picture or pattern on the white paper. Ask the child to press down hard while drawing with the crayon.
2 Gently paint over the top of the picture with the thin black paint. Just like "magic" the paint will not cover the wax.

A bonfire night picture is a particularly good subject for this treatment.

A recipe for handprint paint

This is what you need:

Recipe No. 1
- *Wallpaper paste (without fungicide).*
- *Food colouring or dry powder paint.*
- *A mixing bowl.*
- *A large spoon.*

Help the child to:

1 Mix the wallpaper paste with water until it resembles thick cream. Add a colour and stir well.
2 Use the mixture to hand print or feet print, but do remind little ones not to put fingers covered with handprint paint in their mouths.

This is what you need:

Recipe No. 2
- *10 tablespoons of soapflakes.*
- *10 tablespoons of cold water starch (without borax).*
- *15 tablespoons of cold water.*
- *Dry powder paint or food colouring.*
- *A mixing bowl.*
- *A large spoon.*

Help the child to:

1 Beat all the ingredients together well in the mixing bowl and use for hand or feet printing.

2 Some children seem afraid of getting their hands dirty with handprint paint. A pale or pretty colour helps to overcome this fear. (Other children seem afraid of having clean hands. There is no known cure for this.)

Drips on paper

This is what you need:

- *A sheet of paper.*
- *Different coloured paints.*
- *An assortment of old, unwanted brushes, such as a toothbrush, a nailbrush and a paint brush.*
- *A ruler.*
- *Lots of old newspaper to cover the table top and surrounding area.*
- *An apron.*

Help the child to:

Use the brushes to flick, drip and spray the paint on to the paper. Create spray by scraping the ruler backwards and forwards across the paint-soaked bristles of the toothbrush or nailbrush. Great fun and very, very messy!

Pulled string pictures

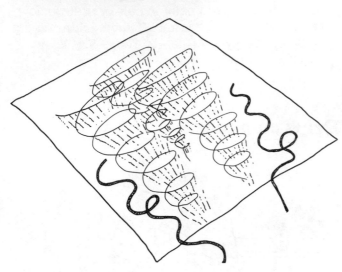

This is what you need:

- *Sheets of paper.*
- *Different coloured paints.*
- *A few pieces of string about 40cm long.*
- *Old newspaper.*

Help the child to:

1 Lay a sheet of paper on to a newspaper-covered table top.
2 Dip a piece of string into some paint until it is completely covered. Gently shake off any drips of paint and then place the string in an interesting shape on top of the paper. Make sure that a small piece of the string hangs just off the sheet of paper.

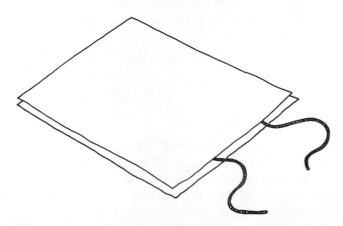

3 Carefully put a second piece of paper on top of the string. Help the child by holding the sheets of paper steady, while she takes hold of the end of the string and gently pulls it out from between the paper.
4 Remove the top sheet of paper and you will see an incredibly delicate pattern underneath. Now dip the string in another colour and start again.

Printing leaves

This is what you need:

- *Sheets of paper.*
- *A collection of leaves, preferably found by the child herself.*
- *Different coloured paints and paint brushes.*

Help the child to:

1 Paint one side of a leaf, trying not to put the paint on too thickly. Then press the leaf carefully on to the paper.
2 Peel the leaf away from the paper. You should see a perfect print of the leaf underneath. Take another leaf and start again.

You could make an Autumn leaf picture by printing with red, orange and yellow paint.

Material and fabric

Hobby-horse

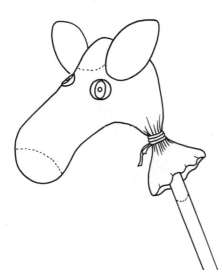

This is what you need:

- *1 old sock.*
- *An old newspaper.*
- *1 garden cane.*
- *String.*
- *Scraps of card or paper.*
- *Glue and a glue brush.*
- *Felt tip pens.*
- *Scissors.*

Help the child to:

1 Stuff the sock with balls of newspaper.
2 Push the garden cane into the sock and tie it securely with string.
3 Draw and cut out two large cardboard eyes and ears.
4 Glue the eyes and ears on to the Hobby-horse.
5 Of course you could make the horse much more elaborate by adding a mane made of wool and a bridle made from strips of cloth. It'll never be any good for the roses though!

Sock puppet

This is what you need:

- *An old sock.*
- *2 buttons.*
- *Scraps of material or felt.*
- *Scraps of wool.*
- *Felt tip pens.*
- *Scissors.*
- *Strong glue and a glue brush.*
- *A piece of card, about 10cm by 20cm.*

Help the child to:

1 Decide what sort of puppet he would like to make. Will it be an animal, a person or even a monster?
2 Cut out ears, a nose, a mouth and other details from the scraps of material or felt. Remember that the two buttons will form the eyes.
3 Lay the sock flat on a table top and slip the piece of card inside it. (This will stretch the fabric and prevent the sock from sticking together.) Glue the eyes and mouth etc into position.
4 When the glue has dried, remove the piece of card from the sock. If you make several sock puppets you could put on a puppet play.

A scarecrow

This is what you need:

- *1 sheet of paper approx 30cms × 30cms.*
- *2 thin sticks or twigs, 1 about 25cm long, the other about 20cms long.*
- *Sellotape.*
- *Glue and a glue brush.*
- *Scissors.*
- *Scraps of material and wool.*
- *Felt tip pens or crayons.*

Help the child to:

1 Stick the twigs down with sellotape on the sheet of paper to form a cross.

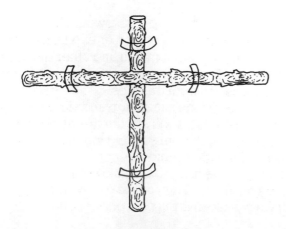

2 Cut out from the material a head, a hat, a jacket and trousers.

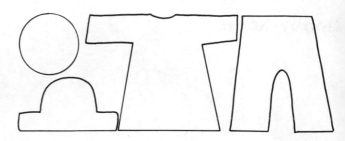

3 Draw a face on the head with the felt tip pens.
4 Glue clothes and head into position on top of the twigs and add tiny pieces of wool to look like straw.

A stocking snake

This is what you need:

- *Old stockings or tights. (If using tights rather than stockings, cut one of the legs off the pair.)*
- *Scissors.*
- *String or rubber bands.*
- *Old newspapers.*
- *Felt tip pens or crayons.*
- *Strong glue and a glue brush.*
- *A sheet of white paper, about 10cm by 10cm.*

Help the child to:

1 Roll up balls of newspaper and stuff these down the stocking.
2 When the stocking is full, fasten the end with a rubber band or piece of string.
3 Draw two eyes on the sheet of paper, cut them out and stick them on to the snake.

Stocking snakes make marvellous draught excluders for underneath doors.

Flour and paint batik

This is what you need:

- *Flour.*
- *Water.*
- *A mixing bowl.*
- *A tablespoon.*
- *An empty washing up liquid bottle.*
- *A paint brush.*
- *A piece of white cotton material. New material must be washed first.*
- *Food colouring or mixed powder paint.*

Help the child to:

1 Put 4 heaped tablespoons of flour into the mixing bowl. Gradually add a little water to the flour until you have a smooth, thick, but pourable mixture.
2 Pour the flour mixture into the washing up liquid bottle and replace the cap.
3 Lay the material on a table top. Squeeze the flour mixture out of the bottle on to the material and create patterns or pictures. If the hole in the cap seems too small, an adult can make it larger with a pair of scissors.
4 When the material has dried completely and the flour mixture has hardened, gently paint all over the surface of the material with the food colouring or paint.

5 When the material has dried for the second time, peel away the dried flour. The flour should have masked the material from the paint, leaving white marks wherever the flour mixture has been.

Dress the boy/girl

This is what you need:

- *A piece of paper, about 30cm by 25cm.*
- *Felt tip pens or crayons.*
- *Scissors.*
- *Strong glue and a glue brush.*
- *Scraps of material and wool.*

Help the child to:

1 Draw the outline shape of a person on the sheet of paper.
2 Use the scraps of materials and cut out a dress or trousers, a hat and coat etc. Stick these on to the body. Very young children will be happy with small odd-shaped pieces of fabric and these can be glued into position on the figure.
3 Hair can be added by gluing scraps of wool round the head, and other details on the face can be drawn with the felt tip pens.

A no-stitch purse

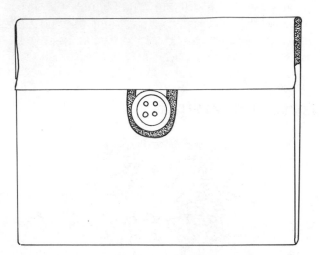

This is what you need:

- *A thin strip of felt, about 10cm by 1cm.*
- *A rectangle of felt, 30cm by 14cm.*
- *1 button.*
- *Strong glue and a glue brush.*
- *Scissors.*

Help the child to:

1 Lay the large rectangle of felt on a table, and fold the felt, bringing one of the short sides up until the bottom edge almost reaches the top, leaving 5cm of felt uncovered. Press the felt firmly with your hand so that it will stay in position.

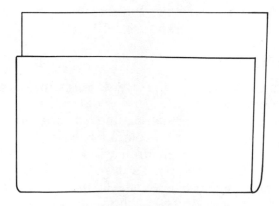

2 Unfold the felt and spread a little glue along both long sides of the rectangle. Remember to stop 5cm from the top and leave the short sides of the rectangle free from glue.

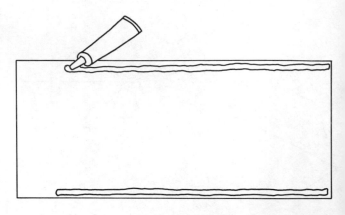

3 Press the glued felt together again. Fold over the top 5cm of felt in order to close the purse with a flap.
4 Glue the button into position in the centre of the purse just a little below the flap of felt.
5 Make a loop with the thin strip of felt and glue this into position under the purse flap. Be sure that the loop sticks out sufficiently to fit round the button.
6 When all the glue has dried, slip the loop of felt over the top of the button to hold the purse shut.

An un-guy

This is what you need:

- *Some old clothes.*
- *Lots of old newspapers.*
- *String.*
- *Safety pins.*
- *1 very large paper bag.*
- *Felt tip pens or crayons.*

Many young children are frightened by the sight of a guy being burnt on a bonfire. So why not make a guy for looking at or sitting on. It doesn't have to be November when you make it, and it doesn't have to be male. A dress and tights can be stuffed with newspaper just as easily. Fasten the guy together with the string or safety pins and make a head by drawing a face on the paper bag. Stuff the bag with newspapers and tie it to the top of the guy's body.

Autumn fruits tie-and-dye

This is what you need:

- *Blackberries or blackcurrants.*
- *A large bowl.*
- *A sieve.*
- *A saucepan.*
- *A wooden spoon.*
- *A piece of white cotton material. An old white handkerchief would do nicely. (New material must be washed first.)*
- *Rubber bands or string.*

Help the child to:

1 Go for a walk and collect the blackberries, but do remind little ones not to eat any berries unless an adult tells them that it is safe to do so.
2 Take the berries home and place them in the saucepan with a little water. Simmer the berries on the stove for 5 minutes and crush them with the wooden spoon as they cook. (Obviously an adult had better do this.)
3 Pour the cooked blackberries through the sieve into the bowl and allow the juice to cool.

4 Take hold of the centre of the material and allow the rest to hang downwards, so that it looks a little like a folded umbrella.

5 Keeping the material in its umbrella shape, start at the pointed end and wrap rubber bands or string tightly around it. Leave a small gap between each rubber band.

6 Dip the material into the blackberry juice until you can no longer see any white material left. Hang the material up to drip dry. When it has dried completely, remove the rubber bands. Unfold the material and you should see a "sun-burst" type pattern in the centre of the material.

Growing things

Potato heads

This is what you need:

- A large round potato.
- A knife.
- A teaspoon.
- Some blu-tack.
- Scissors.
- A sheet of paper.
- Felt tip pens or crayons.
- Mustard and cress seed.

Help the child to:

1 Wash the potato and cut off a slice from each end.
2 Stand the potato on one of its flattened ends and use the teaspoon to scoop out a small hollow in the top of the potato.
3 Use the crayons to draw a nose, eyes, mouth, and ears on the piece of paper and then cut them out. Make a face by sticking the cut-outs on to the potato with blu-tack.
4 Sprinkle a few mustard and cress seeds into the hollow on top of the potato. Keep this moist by adding a few drops of water occasionally and wait for the "Potato Man's" hair to grow.

Rose petal perfume

This is what you need:

- The petals from any fragrant flowers. Beware of any potentially poisonous ones.
- Cold water.
- A sieve.
- A collection of small empty glass bottles with screw tops.
- A potato masher or wooden spoon.
- A large jug.

Help the child to:

1 Put the petals in the large jug. Pour the cold water on to the petals and, using the potato masher or spoon, press the petals until they form a pulp.
2 Leave the mixture to infuse for half an hour and then sieve the liquid into the screw top jars.
3 No one could deny that this is not exactly "Chanel No 5" but little ones feel very proud of their efforts, and mums usually enjoy dabbing a little behind the ears or down the sink.
4 For a really professional finish, design and stick labels on to the bottles. PLEASE NOTE THIS PERFUME WILL NOT KEEP VERY LONG. USE IT WITHIN A COUPLE OF DAYS.

A carrot top jungle

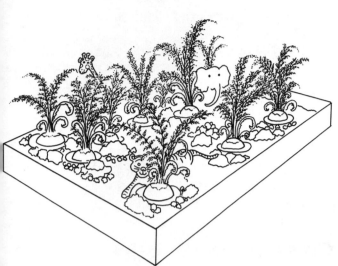

This is what you need:

- As many carrot tops as possible.
- A large shallow container.
- Water.
- A small lid, such as the lid from a meat paste or baby food jar.
- Some 10cm by 10cm pieces of tinfoil. You need as many pieces of foil as you have carrot tops.
- Soil.
- Small stones.
- Pieces of moss.
- Small plastic animals from a toy farm or zoo.

Help the child to:

1 Take a piece of tinfoil and press it tightly round the bottom and sides of the lid. Remove the lid gently and you should be left with a shallow mould. Repeat this until all the tinfoil has been used up.
2 Fill the shallow container with soil and carefully press the tinfoil moulds into the soil. Arrange the small stones and moss around the moulds.
3 Fill the moulds with a little water and put a carrot top in each one. Keep the carrot tops watered and the soil damp and after a few days the carrots will sprout green leaves. Do make sure that the leaves are not eaten – they are likely to make children ill.
4 Now you can put your plastic tiger in the jungle.

Eggshell heads

This is what you need:

- Empty eggshells.
- Felt tip pens.
- Soil.
- Mustard and cress seed.
- 1 teaspoon.
- 1 empty eggbox.
- Scissors.

Help the child to:

1 Cut out the cups from the empty eggbox.
2 Stand an empty eggshell in each cup, open side upwards, and draw a face on each shell with the felt tip pens. The child could also draw buttons or pockets on the cup to represent a body.

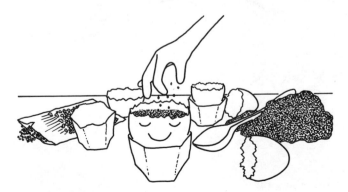

3 Gently spoon a little soil into each shell and sprinkle it with seed. Make sure the soil doesn't dry out and soon the little eggshell men will grow hair. Spot the ones with toupees!

Bulbs in a pot

This is what you need:

- A bulb.
- Bulb fibre or soil.
- A yogurt pot.

Help the child to:

1 Fill the pot with fibre or soil and place the bulb just under the surface of the soil, with the tip of the bulb just showing.
2 Pour a little water into the pot and put it into a very dark cupboard.
3 Look at the pot every day, keep the soil moist and when the first shoots start to appear, take the pot out of the cupboard and put it on to a window ledge.
4 Keep the plant watered and wait for the flower to bloom.

The pot could of course be decorated, but most children usually find enough satisfaction from planting and watching things grow.

Plate garden

This is what you need:

- A large shallow container, such as a tray or plate.
- Soil.
- A teaspoon.
- A garden or outside area in spring or summer.

Help the child to:

1 Go into the garden and fill the shallow container with soil.
2 Collect as many "tiny" flowers, leaves, stones, moss and twigs as you can. Arrange the collection in the soil filled container and create a miniature garden. The stones can form a path, the moss a lawn, the twigs can be trees and so on.
3 You can extend the fantasy if you like with a little hand mirror embedded in the soil to form a pond. Put a lego house in the garden and let toy farm animals eat the grass.

Cress letters

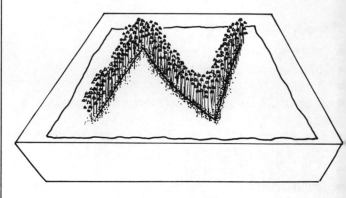

This is what you need:

- A large plate.
- A pencil.
- Blotting paper.
- Mustard and cress seed.
- Water.

Help the child to:

1 Choose a letter or number, it might be his initial e.g. N for Nicholas or his age e.g. 3. Draw the letter or number on to the blotting paper with the pencil.
2 Lay the blotting paper on to the plate and thoroughly dampen it with water.
3 Carefully spread the seeds on to the outline of the letter. Keep the blotting paper damp and watch the cress grow into the chosen initial.

Pressing flowers

This is what you need:

A paper bag.
Some old newspapers or some paper kitchen towel.
Some heavy objects such as books.

Help the child to:

Go for a walk and collect interesting and beautiful leaves and flowers. Put the collection in the paper bag ready to take home. (Now is the time to teach children that certain plants and flowers are rare and some are poisonous. Only the most common flowers should be picked and fingers should never be put near the mouth while handling plants.)
Take the flowers indoors and press them between the sheets of newspaper. Place the heavy weights on top and leave them undisturbed for as long as possible.
Pressed flowers have a multitude of uses. They make marvellous pictures if arranged and stuck on to coloured paper. They can also make very pretty birthday cards and bookmarks.

Acorn in a bottle

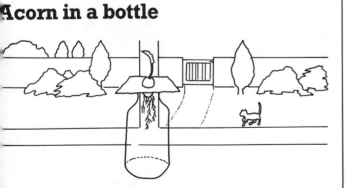

This is what you need:

An empty milk bottle.
A small piece of card, 5cm by 5cm.
Scissors.
An acorn.
Water.

Help the child to:

1 Remove the outer cup from the acorn.
2 Cut a small hole in the middle of the piece of card. Be sure that it is big enough for the acorn to sit snugly in, but not so big that the acorn falls through.
3 Fill the milk bottle right up to the top with water.
4 Put the acorn in the hole in the card and put the card on top of the bottle, so that the pointed end of the acorn is resting in the water. Put the bottle on a window ledge.
5 Keep the bottle topped up with water and you will soon see little roots and green shoots appearing.

Beans in a jar

This is what you need:

- *An empty jam jar.*
- *2 or 3 broad bean seeds.*
- *Blotting paper.*
- *Scissors.*
- *Water.*

Help the child to:

1 Cut the blotting paper so that it fits snugly round the inside of the jam jar.
2 Place the beans between the blotting paper and the side of the jar.
3 Pour a little water into the bottom of the jar and watch the blotting paper soak it up.
4 Keep the paper moist and watch the beans sprouting roots and shoots.

Junk boxes

Trains and cars

This is what you need:

- Lots of large empty cardboard boxes.
- A thick black felt tip pen.
- A long length of thick string.
- Scissors.

Give the child plenty of room and the boxes. The rest is up to him or her. Children love inventing uses for boxes and it would be a pity to spoil imaginative play by suggesting how they might be used. Don't intrude until the child seems ready for some adult involvement.

When the time comes for you to join in, you could help the child to:

1 Make the boxes into cars or spaceships, by drawing wheels, headlights, buttons and levers on the boxes with the felt tip pen.

or

2 Tie the boxes loosely together in a line, by threading thick string through a hole in the back of one box and the front of another. In this way you can make a train.

There is no end to the potential of large empty boxes. They can create anything from a hospital bed for a sick teddy to a deep-sea submarine.

Tambourine

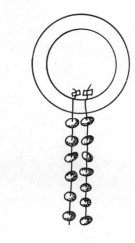

This is what you need:

- The lid from a round container. A margarine, ice-cream or cheese box lid would be suitable.
- 2 pieces of string about 25cm long.
- Milk bottle tops.
- Sellotape.
- Scissors.

Help the child to:

1 Tie a knot on the end of each piece of string.
2 Make a small hole in the centre of each milk bottle top with the scissors. Then thread the tops on to the two pieces of string. Each piece of string should have roughly the same number of tops on it.
3 When you have finished threading, sellotape the strings to the inside rim of the lid.
4 The children can now tap out a tune on the lid with their fingers, or rattle and shake the milk bottle tops.

A box house

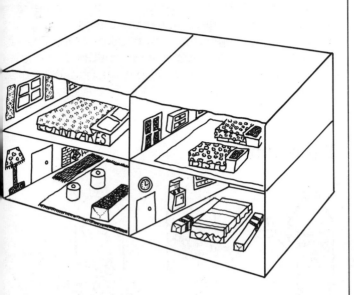

This is what you need:

- *Several large cardboard grocery boxes.*
- *Strong glue and a glue brush.*
- *Scissors.*
- *Old magazines and catalogues.*
- *Scraps of material.*
- *An assortment of smaller cardboard boxes.*
- *A thick felt tip pen.*

Help the child to:

1 Cut any flaps off the large grocery boxes and glue the boxes together, so that all the hollow sides are facing the same way.
2 Look through the old magazines and catalogues and cut out any pictures of furniture and household items you find.
3 Decide which of the "box" rooms will be the kitchen, living room, bedroom and so on. Stick the cut out pictures on to the walls of the appropriate room.
4 More furniture can be made from the smaller cardboard boxes, e.g. an empty tea packet can be the kitchen table. The scraps of material can be turned into bedding and curtains, and other details such as doors and windows can be drawn in with the felt tip pen.

Loo-roll animals

This is what you need:

- *2 pieces of thick card, 8cm by 8cm.*
- *1 toilet roll tube.*
- *Scissors.*
- *Strong glue and a glue brush.*
- *Felt tip pens or crayons.*

Help the child to:

1 Draw the face of a favourite animal on one of the pieces of card, and draw the animal's tail on the other.

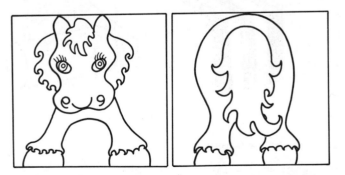

2 Stick the two cards across the ends of the tube with the head at one end and the tail at the other. Make sure that the tube is in the middle of both pieces of card.
3 When the glue has dried, stand the animal up.
4 Make lots of these animals and start your own zoo or farm.

Maracas

This is what you need:

- *An empty washing up liquid bottle.*
- *A handful of dried peas.*
- *A piece of paper. If you are using a large washing up liquid bottle, the paper will need to be 25cm by 30cm.*
- *Sellotape.*
- *Felt tip pens or crayons.*

Help the child to:

1 Remove the top from the washing up liquid bottle and make sure that it is completely empty and dry inside.
2 Draw patterns or pictures on the paper and then sellotape it to the outside of the bottle.
3 Drop the dried peas into the bottle and replace the top. Now shake it. It makes a great noise!

Guitar

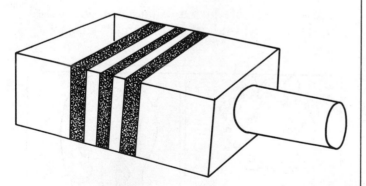

This is what you need:

- *1 empty shoe box without a lid.*
- *Several large thick rubber bands.*
- *1 toilet roll tube.*
- *Strong glue and a glue brush.*

Help the child to:

1 Glue the toilet roll tube on to the end of the shoe box.

2 Wait until the glue has dried and then wrap the elastic bands round the middle of the box. Leave a 1cm space between each of the bands.
3 Your guitar is now ready for plucking! Of course it makes relatively little noise but children love to pretend to be rock and roll stars, especially if they have a pop record to mime to.

Face skittles

This is what you need:

- *Empty washing up liquid bottles.*
- *An old newspaper.*
- *Sellotape.*
- *Felt tip pens or crayons.*
- *A few sheets of paper, 30cm by 22cm. (You need as many sheets of paper as there are bottles.)*

Help the child to:

1 Wrap a sheet of paper round the middle of each bottle and sellotape it into position.
2 Draw a funny face on the front of each bottle.
3 Take a sheet of newspaper and crush it tightly into a ball. Do this until you have at least five balls.
4 Stand the face skittles up in a group and see how many you can knock down with the newspaper balls.

This is obviously a good activity for practising counting.

A television

This is what you need:

- *1 large empty box – a cereal box would do nicely.*
  1 empty eggbox.
  Drinking straws.
  1 sheet of card. This could be taken from yet another empty box.
  Magazines or comics.
- *Glue and a glue brush.*
- *Sellotape.*
- *Scissors.*

Help the child to:

1 Cut out a rectangular hole from the front of the empty box and make a thin slit in the bottom.

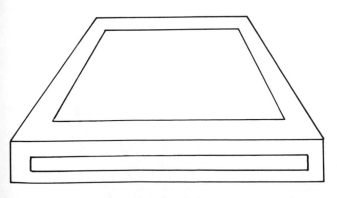

2 Glue a colourful picture from a magazine inside the box, so that you can see it clearly through the hole in the front.

3 Cut out two eggbox cups and stick these on to the front of the box. They make the "on/off" switches.

4 Cut out favourite TV characters or animals and people from the magazines and glue these on to card. When these are dry, cut them out carefully and stick a drinking straw on to the back of each one with sellotape.

5 Pop the characters through the slit in the bottom of the television box and invent stories for them! This is almost certainly how "Dynasty" was written.

Pop-up Punch or Judy

This is what you need:

- *A toilet roll tube.*
- *A piece of white paper, 9cm by 15cm.*
- *1 straw.*
- *1 circle of card, about the size of a 5p.*
- *Felt tip pens or crayons.*
- *Sellotape.*

Help the child to:

1 Sellotape the piece of white paper to the outside of the toilet roll tube. Then draw a headless body on to the paper.

2 Draw a happy face on the cardboard circle and then attach it to the top of the straw with sellotape.

3 Push the straw up through the tube until the face peeps out. Little children love to play "Peep-O" with these figures.

A bottle boat

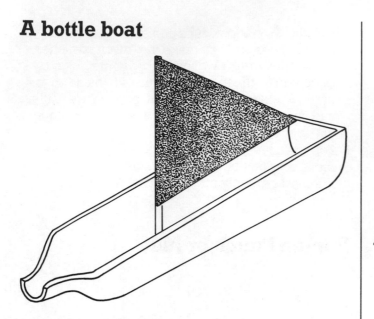

This is what you need:

- *1 empty washing up liquid bottle, or a plastic squash bottle.*
- *Scissors.*
- *1 straw.*
- *1 piece of white paper, 18cm by 18cm.*
- *A ruler.*
- *A pencil.*
- *A small ball of plasticine.*
- *Sellotape.*

Help the child to:

1 Cut the bottle in half along its length. (Obviously an adult had better do this.)
2 Lay the half bottle down on its side and press the ball of plasticine into the middle of the bottom of the boat.

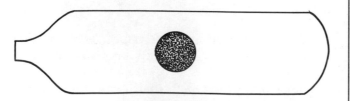

3 Fold the piece of paper in half to make a triangle. Put the straw inside the triangle next to the folded crease, making sure that about 4cm of the straw sticks out of the paper. Sellotape the straw into position.

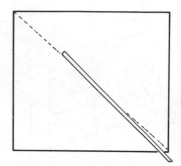

4 Stand the "sail" up in the boat by pushing the straw into the ball of plasticine. Find the nearest bath and organise the launching ceremony. Champagne strictly for the grown-ups.

Caterpillar eggbox

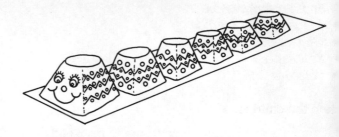

This is what you need:

- *1 strip of card, 5cm by 30cm.*
- *1 empty eggbox.*
- *Scissors.*
- *Strong glue and a glue brush.*
- *Paints or crayons.*

Help the child to:

1 Use the scissors to cut the top off the eggbox and separate the eggbox cups.
2 Use paints or crayons to decorate five of the cups. On the sixth cup draw a face.
3 Starting with the face, stick the cups in a long line on to the strip of card. Of course you could make a much longer caterpillar by using more egg boxes.

A bonfire night rocket

This is what you need:

- *1 toilet roll tube.*
- *1 thin garden cane about 50cm long.*
- *Tinfoil.*
- *Old colourful magazines.*
- *Scissors.*
- *Glue and a glue brush.*
- *Sellotape.*

Help the child to:

1 Cover the tube with tinfoil and sellotape this into position.
2 Carefully sellotape one end of the garden cane inside the tube.
3 Choose some really colourful pictures from the magazines and cut these up into thin strips.
4 Sellotape or glue the magazine strips so they trail from the bottom of the tube.
5 DO remind little ones that real fireworks must NEVER be held in the hand.

Eggbox spiders

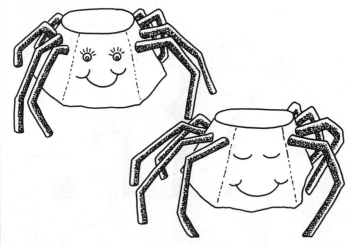

This is what you need:

- *1 empty eggbox.*
- *1 packet of pipe cleaners.*
- *Felt tip pens.*
- *Scissors.*

Help the child to:

1 Cut out one of the eggbox cups.
2 Use the sharp point of the scissors to make eight tiny holes around the outside of the eggcup. Obviously a grown-up had better do this.

3 Use four pipe cleaners. Push each pipe cleaner through a hole on one side of the cup and out through a hole on the opposite side. Bend the pipe cleaners slightly to make them look more like spiders' legs.
4 Draw a spider's face on the front of the eggcup. Then, if you like, add a length of elasticated thread to the top of the cup.

Flowers in a pot

This is what you need:

- An empty yogurt pot.
- A teaspoon.
- Enough soil to fill the yogurt pot.
- A small ball of plasticine.
- 3 pipe cleaners, green ones would be nice.
- Felt tip pens or crayons.
- A small piece of card, 15cm by 20cm.
- Scissors.

Help the child to:

1 Draw three flower shapes on the piece of card. Cut the shapes out and colour them on both sides.

2 Make a small hole with the pointed end of the pair of scissors in the centre of each card flower. (An adult had better do this.)
3 Push the pipe cleaners through the holes in the flowers, leaving about 1cm of pipe cleaner showing on top of each flower.

4 Take the plasticine and make six tiny balls, two for each flower. One ball goes on top of the flower, pressed on to the pipe cleaner. The second one should be pressed around the pipe cleaner just underneath the flower.
5 Using the teaspoon, fill the yogurt pot with soil and stick the three flowers into it. Bend the pipe cleaners slightly for a more natural effect.

Of course the yogurt pots can be decorated to make them look even prettier.

Presents

A desk-tidy for daddy

This is what you need:

- *A toilet roll tube.*
- *A sheet of pretty paper, 17cm by 24cm.*
- *A piece of card, 10cm by 10cm.*
- *Glue and a glue brush.*
- *1 new ballpoint pen or pencil.*
- *Sellotape.*

Help the child to:

1 Wrap the pretty paper round the tube and sellotape it into position. Tuck the loose ends of the paper into the top and bottom of the tube.
2 Glue one end of the tube and press it on to the piece of card. When the tube has dried in this position, pop the pen into its new holder.
3 If you are feeling really ambitious, several tubes could be stuck together on a larger piece of card so that daddy can keep rulers, pencils and all sorts of things tidy.

A cracker of bath salts for aunty

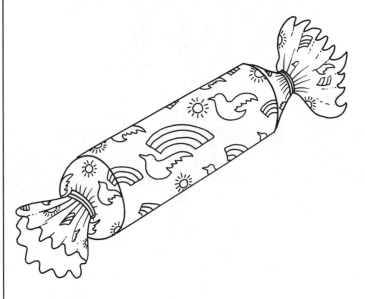

This is what you need:

- *A toilet roll tube.*
- *A small piece of cling film.*
- *A small handful of bath salts.*
- *A piece of pretty wrapping paper, 21cm by 30cm.*
- *Sellotape.*
- *2 rubber bands.*

Help the child to:

1 Take the small handful of bath salts and wrap them in the cling film. Put the wrapped bath salts inside the tube.
2 Wrap the pretty paper round the tube, making sure that an equal amount of paper overlaps each end of the tube. Then sellotape the paper into position.
3 Tie up both ends of the cracker with a rubber band.
4 The cracker can be decorated with a small picture cut out from an old Christmas or birthday card and stuck on to the tube. Alternatively, a simple bow of ribbon could be tied on.

A bookmark for grandad

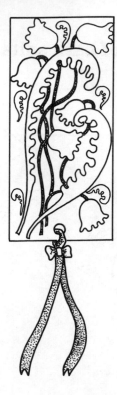

This is what you need:

- *A piece of card, 4cm by 15cm.*
- *A length of thin ribbon, 30cm long.*
- *Clear adhesive film, 16cm by 9cm.*
- *Felt tip pens and crayons or some pressed flowers.*
- *If using pressed flowers you will need glue and a glue brush.*
- *Scissors.*

Help the child to:

1 Decorate the card either by drawing with the crayons or by sticking on the pressed flowers.
2 Cover the card with the adhesive film.
3 With the pointed end of the scissors make a small hole in the bottom edge of the card. (Obviously an adult had better do this.)
4 Thread the ribbon through the hole and tie a knot in it as close to the card as possible. Leave the rest of the ribbon to hang down.

A comb in a case for gran

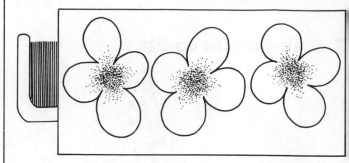

This is what you need:

- *1 piece of felt, 14cm by 14cm.*
- *Strong glue and a glue brush.*
- *3 pieces of felt, each 4cm by 4cm. (Make sure that this felt is a different colour from the larger piece of felt.)*
- *Glitter.*
- *Scissors.*
- *A felt tip pen.*
- *A new comb.*

Help the child to:

1 Fold the large piece of felt in half. Unfold the felt and glue round three of the edges. Fold the felt again and press the glued edges together.

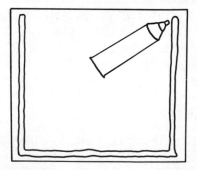

2 Draw and cut out three very simple flower shapes from the smaller pieces of felt. Glue the flowers on to the front of the comb case. Dab a spot of glue in the centre of each flower and sprinkle this with glitter.
3 When the glue has dried pop a new comb inside the case. Guaranteed to please gran!

A pencil case for big brother

This is what you need:

- *A large empty washing-up liquid bottle.*
- *Scissors.*
- *A piece of thin card, 25cm by 20cm.*
- *Sellotape.*
- *2 sheets of coloured paper, approx 17cm by 25cm, and 6cm by 25cm.*
- *Coloured gummed paper.*
- *Crayons.*
- *A few new crayons.*

Help the child to:

1 Cut the bottle in half, 7cm down from the top rim.
2 Gently roll the thin card into a tube shape and drop this into the bottom half of the bottle. The card should protrude slightly.

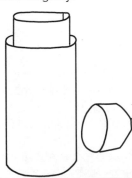

3 Draw pictures and stick gummed shapes on to the two sheets of paper. Wrap the larger sheet round the outside of the bottom half of the bottle and the smaller sheet round the outside of the top half. Sellotape the paper into position.
4 Put a few new crayons into the bottle and put the top back on. The card inside the bottle will hold the top in place.

A set of funny face pencil tops for big sister

This is what you need:

- *3 new pencils.*
- *3 strips of paper, 3cm by 25cm.*
- *3 circles of white card, about the size of a 5p coin.*
- *Felt tip pens or crayons.*
- *3 pieces of double-sided sticky tape or glue.*
- *Sellotape.*

Help the child to:

1 Wrap a paper strip tightly round the top of each pencil and sellotape or glue the strips into position.
2 Draw some funny faces on the card circles and then stick them with the double-sided sticky tape on to the paper covered pencil tops.

A paperweight for uncle

This is what you need:

- *1 large smooth stone from the beach or garden. (The hunt for the stone is half the fun.)*
- *Felt tip pens or paints.*
- *Varnish and a brush to put it on with.*

Help the child to:

1 Wash and dry the stone.
2 Decide which is the top and which is the bottom of the stone. Then draw or paint a picture on the top of the stone. The picture could reflect a favourite hobby or pastime that uncle has, e.g. football.
3 When the paint has dried, apply a coat of varnish for a really professional finish.

A pair of binoculars for a friend

This is what you need:

- *2 empty toilet roll tubes.*
- *Sellotape.*
- *Scissors.*
- *A length of string or ribbon, 50cm long.*
- *2 round cellophane jam pot covers. The slightly coloured ones make using the binoculars more interesting.*
- *2 elastic bands.*

Help the child to:

1 Stretch a jam pot cover over one end of each toilet roll tube. Push an elastic band over each tube to hold the cellophane covers in position.
2 Lay the tubes side by side so that the covered ends are next to each other. The tubes are held in this position by wrapping a length of sellotape around them.
3 In order to make the strap for the binoculars an adult should make a small hole with the scissors at the top end of each tube, i.e. opposite the cellophane covered end. Thread and knot the string through the holes.

A rattle for baby

This is what you need:

- *5 or 6 empty cotton reels.*
- *A piece of clean string approx 35cm long.*

Help the child to:

1 Wash the cotton reels and dry them.
2 Thread the cotton reels on to the piece of string. Then tie the two ends of the string together in a strong knot.
3 The rattle makes a good present for a child to give to a new brother or sister.

A birthday balloon card

This is what you need:

- *A piece of thick card 40cm by 24cm.*
- *A felt tip pen.*
- *Crayons.*
- *Sharp scissors to be used by an adult.*
- *A balloon.*

Help the child to:

1 Fold the card in half so that the front of the card measures 20cm by 24cm. Write a birthday message inside the card.
2 Draw and colour a large happy clown's face on the front of the card.
3 Using the scissors, make a small hole in one corner of the clown's mouth. Obviously an adult had better do this.
4 The balloon can now be blown up (not too fully)

and the knotted end inserted through the hole. Of course the card can be sent with the balloon deflated and merely threaded through the hole. Then the recipient can blow the balloon up for herself.

A seed coaster for mummy's coffee cup

This is what you need:

- *A jam jar or coffee jar lid.*
- *A small amount of mixed waterproof filler.*
- *A teaspoon.*
- *A blunt knife.*
- *Dried peas, lentils and rice.*
- *Silver or gold spray.*

Help the child to:

1 Use the teaspoon to fill the lid with filler. Then smooth the surface of the filler with the knife.
2 Press the dried seeds into the filler. Be sure that the seeds are pressed down well.
3 When the filler has dried, shake off any loose seeds and spray the coaster all over with gold or silver spray. Alternatively the seeds could be varnished.